Our Global Village

France

Written by: Ann Edmonds
Illustrated by: Ada K. Hanlon

Milliken Publishing Company St. Louis, Missouri

To the children, parents, and teachers at *La Bibliotheque Americaine, St. Agnes maternelle, et la classe de Marie–Claude and Katherine, La Perrusaie,* all of Angers, France. *Merci beaucoup!*

Milliken Publishing Company
1100 Research Boulevard
St. Louis, MO 63132

Managing Editor: Kathy Hilmes

ISBN 0-7877-0042-8

A Multicultural Experience

Our Global Village hopes to share ideas, hands–on activities, and resources from other cultures which will lead you, your students, and their families in different experiences. Learning how others live, think, and react is becoming increasingly important. The earth is a global village, and each of us is quickly affected by events, styles, disasters, and ideas from far away. Old barriers of mountains and oceans are disappearing because of fax machines and airplanes. It is important to help young children learn about and value the diversity in the world around them. Fortunate is the child who has the opportunity to interact with people who speak different languages, who eat different foods, and whose skins are different colors. This child will come to appreciate the fascinating differences between people in the world while learning that people are much the same. We hope this resource series will help create a multicultural community in your classroom as you learn and share different languages, customs, and celebrations.

Table of Contents

UNITED KINGDOM
BELGIUM
GERMANY
English Channel
LUXEMBOURG
CHANNEL
ISLANDS (U.K.)
Normandy
Lorraine
Paris
Versailles
Brittany
LeMans
Orléans
Champagne
Angers
SWITZERLAND
Anjou
Tours
Burgundy
Nanterre
Bobigny
Paris
Creteil
Ile-de-France
Lyon
ITALY
Limoges
Bordeaux
Lascaux
Provence
Nice
MONACO
Bay of Biscay
Toulouse
Marseille
Basque Region
Gulf of Lions
ANDORRA
SPAIN
CORSICA
FRANCE

France

France is the largest country in western Europe. In both manufacturing and trade, France is a world leader. Citizens are guaranteed free national health care and education. Population shifts from northern Africa and eastern Europe continue to affect French society and economy. Currently, France exports food and energy, as well as agricultural and manufactured goods, to countries in the European Union. France's culture and language have influenced the world for centuries. The natural beauty and richness of France is famous throughout the world. Tourism enhances the economy as people come to marvel at art collections, wander through towns of ancient to very modern architecture, indulge in fabulous meals, and view the gorgeous scenery.

France has a close relationship with the United States. Economically, politically, and militarily, the two countries have had a long, and occasionally turbulent, connection. During the early 1600s, French voyagers, fur trappers, nuns, and priests made the trip across the Atlantic Ocean to America. Philosophers of the French Enlightenment influenced Thomas Jefferson, John Adams, and other Americans who wrote the Declaration of Independence and the U.S. Constitution. The Marquis de LaFayette and other Frenchmen fought for the Colonies in the American Revolution. During WWI and WWII, American soldiers fought for France in the trenches and on the beaches of Normandy. The Statue of Liberty in New York was a gift from France celebrating 100 years of freedom; a smaller version of the statue—a gift from the U.S. to France—nestles along the Seine River. Each year, North American and French students study each other's language and culture in cities across the United States and France. France and the United States are connected through years of common need and interest.

Area—552,000 square kilometers (213,000 square miles)

Form of Government—Democratic republic

Flag—*Le Tricolore,* the French flag, is composed of three vertical panels of blue, white, and red.

National Anthem—*"Le Marseillaise."* The national anthem was written during the French Revolution.

Population—About 57 million. One–sixth of the people live in the capital city of Paris.

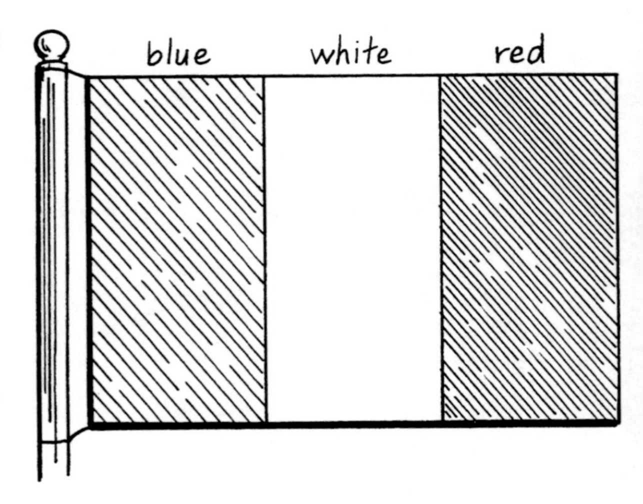

Other highly populated cities include Marseille, Lyon, Toulouse, and Nice. Immigrants comprise 7% of the population and come from Algeria, Morocco, Tunisia, Italy, Portugal, Spain, Turkey, and Indochina.

Geographical Regions—Mediterranean areas, Pyrenees Mountains near Spain, Alps and Jura mountains near Switzerland, Central Highlands, Aquitanian Lowlands, Rhine River Valley and Vosges Mountains near Germany, Northeast Plateau near Belgium, northern plains, Brittany–Normandy Hills near the Atlantic coast, and Corsica, an island near Italy.

Climate—Most of France experiences moderately warm summers and mild, cool winters, with mild precipitation all year. In the south of France by the Mediterranean Sea, however, summers are hot and dry. The famous mistral winds—winds that blow across France from the Atlantic—blow cold and strong in the winter. On the Atlantic side, the weather is milder with much rain. Inland, the climate changes with the seasons.

Language—French. The dialect spoken in Paris became standard French in the 1500s. Breton, spoken in Brittany, and Basque, spoken near the Pyrenees, are two other languages spoken in France. *L'Académie Française* (The French Academy), a prestigious academic institution, is in charge of keeping the national language accurate and purged of non–French words. The French language is highly prized as the "essence of being French."

Religion—75% Roman Catholic, 3% Muslim, 2% Protestant, 1% Jewish. The remaining people are atheist or have no strong religious beliefs.

Money—1 franc = 100 centimes. Francs are decorated with the faces of artists, scientists, musicians, and other cultural icons. For example, the 10 franc note features Berlioz, the composer, and the 50 franc note features Corneille, a 17th century playwright.

In Your Classroom

Arrange a research area: Explore France! Begin to collect books—in English and French—about France. Pictures of France, famous French, and French contributions can be found in books of art, history (including biographies), literature, and music. Introduce France with a display of photography, art, and picture books. Display some books with castles, knights, and troubadours pictured. Add picture dictionaries to your area for reference. *(See Additional Resources for selected titles.)*

Display a world map or globe. Help students find France on the European continent. Where is France in relation to your classroom? Help students to calculate this distance in kilometers/miles.

Distribute maps of France. Note that France is a hexagon—roughly the size of Texas—and discuss France's proximity to other European countries, and to Africa. Discuss how France's geographical position and natural features, such as mountains, have affected its history, language, and culture, as well as its weather. Would France would be a good neighbor? What might you guess about France based on its geography and fertile land?

All nations have icons that celebrate the culture and educate others about the nation's history. Just as the United States' flag, Uncle Sam, and the Statue of Liberty represent the United States, the *tricolore,* the proud rooster, and royal designs such as the *fleur de lis* represent France. Can students think of other symbols of France and/or the U.S.? As they continue studying France, ask students to note how national symbols are woven into stories, art, architecture, and games.

One of the most flamboyant and well–known symbols of France is the 320–meter–high Eiffel Tower in Paris. Built in 1889, it was the world's tallest building for over four decades. Create a bulletin board by outlining the Eiffel Tower on 2 meters of butcher paper. Title the display, *"La Belle France"* (Beautiful France). As students learn about France, have them fill in the outline with pictures, news clippings, and facts.

History

France has a long, illustrious history which is a source of pride for the French people. History pervades the culture and its influence can be seen in France's architecture, urban planning, food, literature, and arts, as well as in its politics and economics. Although the old is highly respected, new ways and new styles are also admired.

Early History

The area now known as France was settled over a period of centuries by many different peoples. The earliest settlers were the Gauls, a Celtic group who settled in the rich northern region. In later years, Norsemen (Vikings) raided in the north, most noticeably around Normandy, the northern coast of France. They occupied some areas and weakened the Gauls.

Led by Julius Caesar, the Romans defeated the Gauls (58 B.C.–51 B.C.) and added the territory to the Roman Empire. Roman law, Roman roads, and the Roman language of Latin formed the framework for much of modern France's infrastructure, judiciary system, and language. The popular, modern cartoon character, Asterix, continues the "war" between Gauls and Romans.

The Amphitheater of Nîmes, built by Romans nearly 2000 years ago

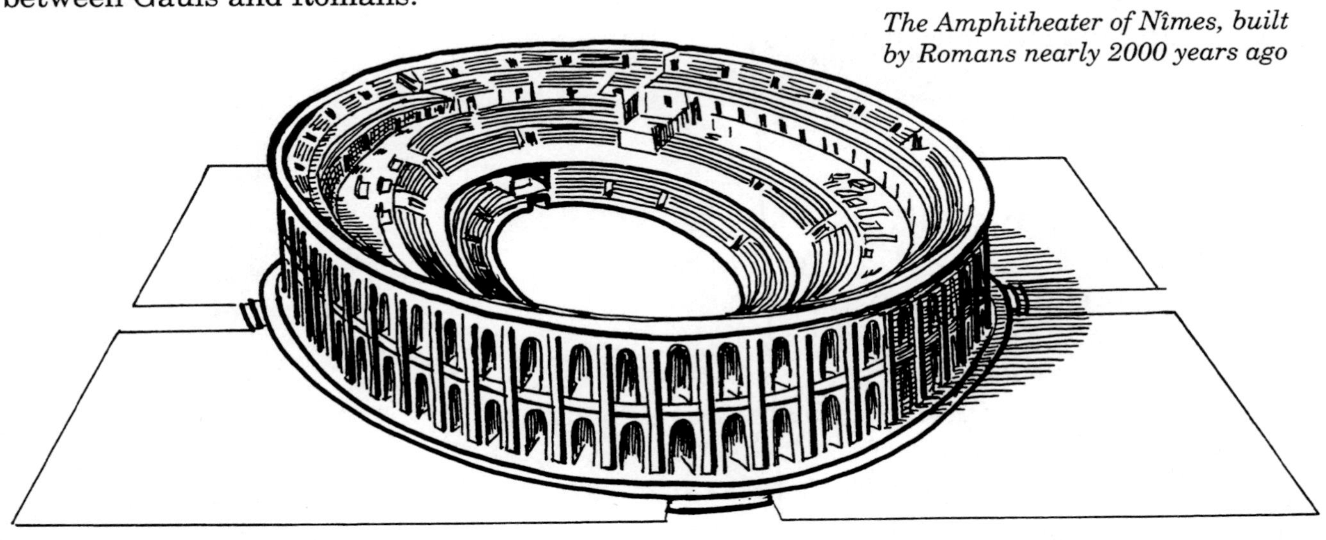

After the collapse of the Roman Empire around 400 A.D., barbaric Germanic tribes invaded Europe. The Franks inhabited the territory of France and gave France its name. In 486 A.D., Clovis, King of the Franks, introduced Christianity to the region. He expanded France's territory and, after his death, his kingdom was divided among his three sons, as was the tradition.

In the 700s, the Moors from North Africa conquered Spain and attacked France, bringing Islam to southern Europe. Fighting in the name of Christianity, Charles the Hammer defeated these Arabs in the famous Battle of Tours, blocking their path through Europe. His son, Pepin the Short, became ruler in 751, and expanded the Frankish Kingdom. This was the beginning of the Carolingian Dynasty.

The most famous of all Frankish kings was Charlemagne (Charles the Great), son of Pepin the Short. He expanded France's borders to include most of western Europe, creating the largest empire since the Roman Empire. He was crowned Holy Roman Emperor by the pope in 800. During his reign, Charlemagne opened schools for clergy and teachers, set up regular courts whose judgments were based on common laws, improved farming techniques, and coined money. He gave large tracts of land to nobles, and in exchange, they supported him politically and militarily. The nobles also repaired and maintained bridges, roads, and defenses on their land. This type of arrangement is called *feudalism.*

During the Capetian Dynasty, which followed Charlemagne's death, the economy, as well as towns along major trade routes, began to thrive again. Craft workers joined together to form guilds and became a politically and economically powerful middle class in towns. Although some people moved to towns to look for jobs, the population remained largely rural. Agricultural techniques were too primitive to support a large population of non–agricultural workers. Slowly, France evolved from a loose union of powerful feudal states into a centralized monarchy. Norsemen again invaded France, and this time captured Normandy, as well as Anglo–Saxon England (1066). England was France's enemy, and now that the two were united, the stage was set for the intermittent battles of the 100 Years' War (1337–1453).

Joan of Arc, Maid of Orléans

The Growth of France

In 1328, Charles IV died without a male heir and the Capetian Dynasty ended. One of his cousins, Philip VI, took the throne, and thus began the Valois Dynasty. This dynasty endured the 100 Years' War, as France battled England to keep "fair France." The saving grace for France was a young peasant girl who heard voices from God urging her to lead French soldiers against the English. With the armor, weapons, and horse given to her by a French prince, Joan of Arc drove the English out of France. When it was discovered she was female, Joan was captured and sold to England. The church burnt her at the stake as a witch. Despite this end, Joan of Arc became one of France's greatest heroes.

In the 1400s and 1500s, the Renaissance influenced and encouraged the creation of great art, literature, and architecture. France became a center for art, fashion, architecture, music, and theater. During this time, royalty, nobility, and the clergy gained immense wealth and power throughout France. However, civil war soon erupted. A well–educated German monk, Martin Luther, spoke out against the abuses of the Catholic Church. His ideas spread over Europe and ignited the Protestant Reformation. In France, Catholics and Protestants (known as Huguenots) fought bitterly, and again, France was war–torn.

Religious struggles continued until the leader of the Huguenots became King Henry IV, the King of France. Henry IV pledged to make France the greatest nation in Europe. He began by building new roads and bridges. His grandson, Louis XIV, known as the Sun King, continued his grandfather's vision of a great French nation. For royal glory, he had the largest and most elaborate palace in the world built in Versailles. He also established trading posts in India and North Africa to bring silks, spices, and exotic treasures to France, and he fought countries all over the globe for land. To support his extravagant ventures, he heavily taxed the common people who struggled to survive. They became increasingly dissatisfied.

The French Revolution

Napoleon Bonaparte, the greatest military genius of his time

The 18th century brought revolutionary ideas and a bloody revolution. French thinkers, particularly *Les Philosophes,* inspired revolutionary thinkers in England's American Colonies. When the Colonies declared themselves to be an independent nation—the United States of America—a French general, the Marquis de LaFayette, went to help win their War of Independence. He then returned to France to aid his own people in their revolt against the upper classes.

In Paris, on July 14, 1789, angry mobs of the middle and lower classes stormed the Bastille, a royal prison, which was the beginning of the French Revolution. It was a Reign of Terror as the common people publicly beheaded tens of thousands of royalty, nobility, and clergy. The guillotine, an efficient beheading machine, became a tool for destroying the monarchy and building a democracy.

In 1799, Napoleon Bonaparte, a young general from Corsica, ended the Reign of Terror by taking control of France. By 1814, Napoleon had implemented a strong central government, a secular legal system, and an efficient military system in France. To build an empire, he conquered much of western and central Europe. Disastrous campaigns in Egypt and Russia, plus the growing power of France's neighbors led to his eventual downfall.

Modern France

The 20th century brought the devastating invasions and battles of WWI and WWII to France. Both wars were heavily fought on French soil. The victorious French of WWI were quickly defeated in WWII by Germany. The Germans along with *des collaborateurs* (French citizens who sided with the Germans) governed France until the Allies freed Paris in 1944. General Charles de Gaulle successfully led *la Résistance* against the Germans and *des collaborateurs.*

After WWII, General de Gaulle became president of the French Republic and established France as an important force during the Cold War era. In the 1950s, the colonies in Indochina, which France had acquired a hundred years earlier, rebelled. Both Vietnam and Algeria fought for—and won—their independence. In spite of the damage caused by world wars and colonial struggles, France's economy continued to grow and the political system remained stable.

Currently, France is a leader in the European Union (European Common Market)—an organization created to remove barriers to the movement of goods, workers, capital, and services among members. France continues to export goods to countries in the Union and around the world. Its main agricultural exports are fruits, grains, wines, cheeses, and perfumes. France also exports industrial products such as cars, nuclear power and machinery, and cultural products such as films, fashion, architecture, and literature.

France's countryside, cityscapes, literature, art, and music are filled with images, memories, and artifacts from the grand history of the country. Throughout France, layers of history remind those in the present of the glory of France.

In Your Classroom

Make a time line on shelving or computer paper. Mark important dates in French history with pictures and drawings.

Design posters describing French heroes like Charlemagne, Joan of Arc, the Sun King, the Marquis de LaFayette, Napoleon, and Charles de Gaulle.

Play "Go Fish," using superstars of French history. Divide the class into groups and have each group choose a superstar to study. After doing research, each group should write the four most important facts about the French superstar. Cut file folders into nine rectangles each, and have the class use them to create a set of Star Cards. They should write one fact on each card and illustrate it. Shuffle all of the cards and play Star Cards like Go Fish.

Castles and Cathedrals

French *châteaux* (castles) come in all shapes and sizes. Huge and elegant castles like Versailles and small stone castles on the Rhône River and in the Loire Valley make the French landscape picturesque. Castles were first built to protect inhabitants from invading armies. Livestock, food, water supplies, families, and servants would crowd in the area protected by stone walls and a moat. Inside were dungeons and towers, feasting halls and narrow hallways. After many years, the castles were transformed into elegant and expensive palaces, and eventually into public places. The Louvre Museum is an excellent example of a castle fortress that became a palace, and later a museum and park.

Awe–inspiring French cathedrals are another way to study French history and culture.

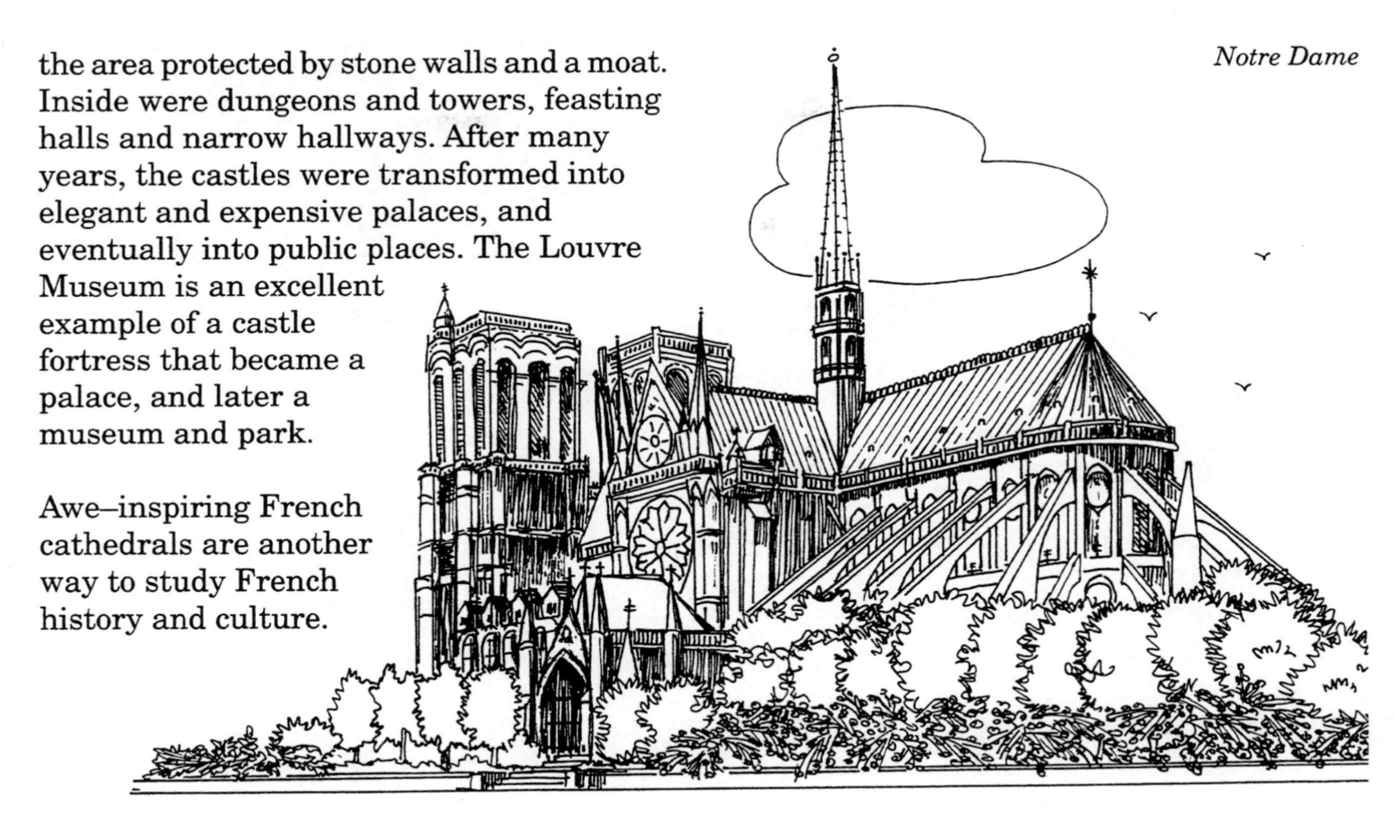

Notre Dame

Heavy stone fortress–like cathedrals were built as the first monuments to God. Then, slightly less massive Gothic cathedrals such as Notre Dame and Rheims were created. Eventually, more elegant structures like Sainte Chapelle were built. Each cathedral is a collection of buildings, built over years and sometimes centuries. Technological advances allowed for wider windows, higher walls, grander arches and domes, and more intricately decorated interiors.

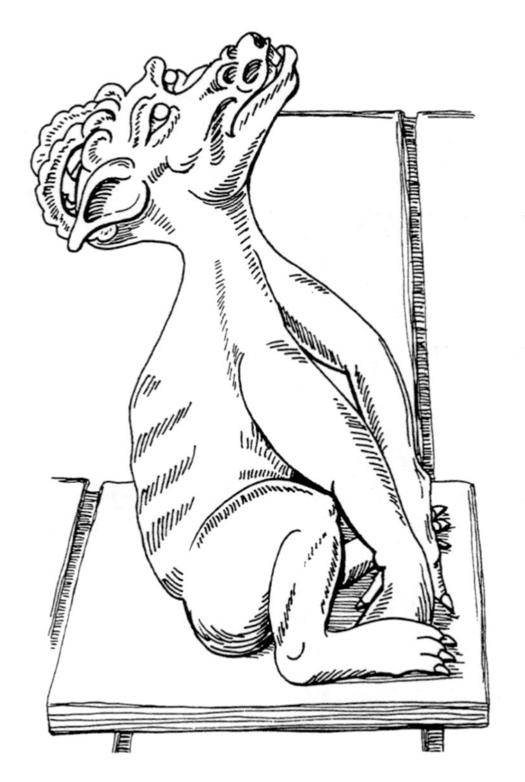

In Your Classroom

Make your own castle with blocks or with sand. Create sturdy castle walls from shoe boxes, oatmeal cylinders, and juice cans. Fly pennants with symbols of royalty. Make sure there is a place for everyone to fit in the protected world of the castle.

Gargoyles decorate the eaves and corners of most cathedrals. Some say their horrid faces scare away evil spirits. Others say gargoyles represent real persons who did not pay the sculptors. Still others say that the gargoyles were just a fashion or decorative twist. Observe gargoyles in pictures or on buildings in your community. Make your own gargoyles from modelling clay. Design gargoyle masks for Mardi Gras. Write a story about a person who could not pay sculptors and who was frozen in stone as a gargoyle.

Holidays and Festivals

In France, festivals give families and communities the opportunity to celebrate historic events, and religious and cultural traditions. Elaborate foods and decorations are prepared, and traditional games are played.

Feast of the Epiphany—January 6 is a Christian holiday celebrating the arrival of the Three Wise Men to Bethlehem to visit the infant Jesus. *La Galette des Rois* (The Cake of Kings) is eaten and *Tirer le Roi!* (Grab the King!) is played. Epiphany continues the feasting of Christmas. People eat sweets and exchange gifts.

Mardi Gras (Fat Tuesday)—This holiday in late February or early March traditionally heralded the Christian fasting season of Lent. The French make crêpes and cakes to deliciously and usefully finish up the flour, butter, eggs and other "fat" ingredients in the house. People dress in elaborate costumes, wear masks, and parade through the streets.

Poisson d'Avril (April Fish Day)—April 1 is a fun festival like April Fool's Day. On this day, the French must beware of silly announcements in the newspapers, on TV, or from friends. People eat chocolates shaped like fish.

May Day—May 1 is a special day that traditionally honors Mary, mother of Jesus. Children sell or give lily of the valley flowers to others. Many people eat chocolates, cakes, and cookies shaped like lilies of the valley.

Bastille Day—July 14 celebrates the fall of the Bastille in 1789, which began the French Revolution. It is celebrated much like Independence Day in the United States. It is a day when the French glory in the past, fly the flag, sing the national anthem, shoot fireworks, and march in parades.

Saint Nicholas' Eve—During the night of December 5, small presents and candies are sometimes left for good boys and girls by Saint Nicholas, the patron saint of children.

Noël (Christmas)—December 25 is a Christian holiday. On December 24, Christmas Eve, the French solemnly commemorate the birth of Jesus by going to church for a Midnight Mass. Late in the night, adults share a feast. While children sleep, *Père Noël* (Father Christmas) visits and brings toys and presents. On Christmas Day, the family gathers together for another splendid feast. Between December 25 and January 6, the French visit friends and family throughout the country. As usual for France, bakeries and chocolatiers are filled with exquisite, seasonal specialities.

In every town and village, people celebrate local holidays. Local holidays are devoted to a patron saint, commemorate a military victory, or celebrate a legend. On the special day, streets close, merchants offer sales, and people gather to watch local legends acted out on stage or in a parade. Children participate in the performances. Through the festivities, they learn about their heritage and have a great time with family and friends.

Père Noël, Father Christmas

In Your Classroom

For the Epiphany, play the game, Grab the King! To prepare for the game, outline a pizza round (or other circle) on poster paper. You will need a circle for every eight children. On copier or construction paper, outline and cut out the same number of circles. Then cut these into eight pie–shaped pieces, and distribute them so that the children can decorate them. Locate dice marked with dots, numbers, colors, or shapes (one die for each group of eight), and have children include these markings on their pie pieces. Collect the pieces and lay them on top of the poster–paper circles. Mark one piece on each circle as the *fève*. The *fève* is the winning piece of cake. Whoever receives it should be crowned as king or queen for the day.

To play the game, give each group of eight children one game set (poster–paper circle, eight pieces, one die). They should take turns rolling the die and "serving" themselves the piece of cake indicated. The child who pulls the *fève* wins. He or she is crowned king or queen and should be awarded special privileges all day. The king or queen will have *bonne chance,* or good luck, all year.

Explain the origins of *Poisson d'Avril* (April Fool's Day): In the 600s, the calendar that people used began on April 1—that was the first day of the new year. But there were not enough days on the calendar to match the solar year, so dates were mixed up. Pope

Gregory changed the calendar to fix it. On the new calendar, the first day of the new year was January 1. Some people forgot this, and they would celebrate the new year on April 1—April Fools' Day. They were like fish out of water!

Make April Fish to hang in your windows. Have students draw a simple fish shape on large construction paper. (You may want to provide a pattern for them to trace.) They can then decorate the fish with gentle watercolors or flashy acrylics. Remind students to add eyes, gills, scales, and fins. Cut out the fish and hang them on the bulletin board or in the window. Make a spring pond scene. Alternatively, fasten string to the head and let students fly their fish—fish out of water make quite a splash!

To celebrate Mardi Gras, make crêpes or cakes *(see Fabulous Foods)*. Have a family night to wear masks, display French projects, and eat French foods.

Mardi Gras is celebrated in many countries around the world. In the United States, the biggest celebration is held in New Orleans, Louisiana. Help students discover the Mardi Gras traditions in your community. Ask them to discover how the holiday is celebrated in Spain, Brazil, and other countries. They might be able to find pictures at the library of carnival games, floats, and costumes.

Help your class make their own Mardi Gras masks. Cut file folders to fit over the eyes and top of the head, and cut out eye holes (or provide inexpensive eye masks). Tape craft sticks to the backs of the masks. Ask children to decide what kind of creatures their carnival masks will represent. Will they be of real or imaginary animals? Then provide them with staplers, glue, scissors, and masking tape, as well as construction paper, markers, feathers, sequins, glitter, and other decorating materials. When the masks are complete, have a parade with them.

On May Day, have children make lily of the valley cards. Show children pictures of lilies of the valley. Then give each child a piece of green construction paper to fold into a card. They can use the center fold of the card as the flower stalk and glue cotton balls onto the card as "bells." You may want to splash a little lily of the valley cologne on the cotton balls.

Make flower cookies using the Cat's Tongue recipe *(see Fabulous Foods)*. Decorate the cookies with candied rose petals or violets, or sprinkle them with colored sugars.

For Bastille Day, play a recording of the French national anthem, *"Le Marseillaise."* Let children use construction paper to make tiny *tricolores* (French flags). They could glue these to toothpick flag poles. Serve cheese or meat sandwiches on baguettes. Read aloud French books like the Madeline or Babar books. Show videos like the *Red Balloon, Asterix,* or *Charles Perrault's Fairy Tales.* Discuss the beginning of the French Revolution in 1789, and compare it to the American Revolution.

For Noël, help children discover Christmas customs around the world. Provide materials for them to design and make cards illustrating the customs.

Daily Life

The typical day of a French child is heavily scheduled and includes several regular mealtimes. School, of course, dominates the week day. Schools meet daily, 9–12, then close for a lunch break from 12–2. During this break, children can stay at school for lunch or return home to eat with their families. Either way, they eat a four– or five–course meal. Dismissal after lunch varies depending on the grade level. Wednesdays and Saturdays are half days. Wednesday afternoon is the time for extracurricular activities like soccer or gymnastics. Some schools still require uniforms, but in most schools, girls wear dresses and boys wear shorts. Children usually wear slippers or leather shoes inside the school. Sports shoes are expensive and are only used for outside games or organized sports. Younger children often wear smocks to protect their clothing. Children walk or ride public transportation to school. There is little parent involvement in the school room, and teacher–parent conferences are rare. Family and school have separate and equally important responsibilities so that the child will be properly educated to be a competent French adult.

The national education system, headed by *le Ministre d'Education,* designs curriculum, educates teachers, and handles school finances all over France. In addition to public schools, there are many private and primarily religious schools. From age 2 through 18, education is free. Children attend *école maternelle* (elementary school) from ages 6 through 12, then they attend *collège* (middle school) and later *lyceé* (high school). Students choose either a vocational or pre–baccalaureat (college preparatory) high school. The "bac" is so difficult to earn that often only 2/3 of students taking the final examination for the degree pass. There are over 75 public universities in France, plus many more private ones. The *Sorbonne* in Paris has been the seat of French intellectual thought since it was founded in 1253. Today it is well regarded throughout the world. The big schools are even more selective than other universities. The educational system in France is standardized with the express goal of preparing competent and highly literate citizens for France. As members of the European Union, French people are valued as well–educated employees.

Les vacances, or vacation time, offers French children and their families time to explore their beautiful country, as well as to travel to other places. Schools close for several two– to three–week blocks in fall, winter, and spring. Adults are allowed five weeks a year paid holiday plus time off for national holidays like Bastille Day. Families often go away from home for a month at a time, especially during the summer. Summer vacation is spent at the beach, in the mountains, in the country, or travelling throughout Europe. Second and third foreign languages are encouraged at French schools and children use the languages regularly.

French families are very close and spend a lot of time together. Children are considered to be an important part of the extended and nuclear family. Families eat together daily, and on weekends, big meals provide the center of activity for the extended family. On a typical Sunday, families shop for and prepare a full meal. Meals can last 3 hours or more. The meal begins with an *aperitif* and *hors d'oeuvres* (pre–dinner drink and appetizers). Then the *entrée* (main course) is served, followed by the *plat principal* (meat or fish course). Next comes the *salade* (salad course), *fromage* (cheese course), *dessert* (pastry or fruit course), and *digestif* (after–dinner drink). After the meal, the family goes out for a walk in the park, around the local castle, or just in the neighborhood. Later, the whole family watches TV or videos, or plays video games. Holidays mean even more cooking and eating and celebrating with family.

Most French people live in cities and towns. Few still live on farms. Appliances and room space are smaller in French homes than in the average American home. Machines are more energy efficient than in the United States. The French can choose ultra–modern or quite ancient houses or apartments. People are less transient in France than in the United States. Rural roots are important, and many families return to the countryside for the holidays. Paris remains the hub of the country, as it has been for centuries, but each city and village maintains its character and a reputation that is proudly shown.

The transportation system is swift and efficient. The TGV *(Train à Grande Vitesse)*—a very high speed train which connects different parts of France—is the world's fastest train. It rides so smoothly that while riding it one can read, nap, and even write without a problem. Buses, cars, and bicycles share the roads. The *Metro,* or subway, makes moving around Paris quick and cheap. Parking is not easy to find anywhere in France because many narrow streets remain from the days before automobiles. On rivers and canals, barges still move slowly, carrying vacationers or cargo. At ports like Marseille, ocean–crossing ships bring in huge loads of imported raw materials. Fishing villages on each coast are filled with luxury boats, as well as working boats. Now that the Chunnel—a tunnel that crosses under the English Channel—is open, people can travel by bus or car between France and the United Kingdom. Walking remains a constant means of transportation in France for both work and pleasure.

Plants and Animals

In France, an amazing 90 percent of the land is fertile! The abundant and diverse plants and animals thriving on the land are important to French culture. Each region of France has food specialties harvested from the land. In Brittany and Normandy, apple ciders and cheeses are produced. Seafood is harvested from the North Atlantic and from the Mediterranean. Beef, poultry, pork, veal, and lamb are all raised carefully to suit the French palate; they are perfectly matched with fruits and vegetables grown in the Loire Valley. Farmers all over France take their work very seriously in this land where good and fresh food is considered vital. They grow enough to fill the nation's market baskets.

Grape vines, mainly in the south and southeast of France, produce world–famous wines. Each region has its own special grapes and wines. Some famous wine regions are Bordeaux, Loire, Anjou, Burgundy, and Champagne. Wine is drunk with meals and is considered part of eating well. It is a vital part of France's economy and culture.

In the south of France, jasmine, geraniums, violets, roses, and bitter orange trees contribute to the ancient perfume industry. They create lavish fields of color. Herbs flourish with the flowers and are used to season foods. Herbs are essential in French cooking. They are inexpensive, interesting, and delicious. Some herbs important to the French are listed below:

ROSEMARY is a spiky small green bush with pale purple flowers. It is used to season lamb, is tasty in teas, and invigorating in baths. Put twigs in your hair, and you will remember important facts: rosemary is called "the herb of remembrance."

TARRAGON has soft, green, thin leaves on a winding bush. It is delicious with fish and chicken. The French call it *"Esdragon,"* which means means "little dragon," because the roots of tarragon can take over a garden and the curly leaves look like escaping coils of smoke and fire.

LAVENDER is a tall, thin, flowering plant. Its purple flowers are used to scent soaps, perfumes, and sachets. Its smell and color are considered typical of southern France.

MINT includes spearmint, peppermint, lemon mint, and other varieties. It is fast–growing and useful to flavor drinks and sweets, to ward off mice, to soothe upset stomachs, and to keep rooms fresh smelling. Mint has been used for centuries in France.

ROSES, queens of flowers, are essential to the French perfume industry. Acres of petals are used to create tiny vials of scent. Roses have inspired stories like *Beauty and the Beast* and *Sleeping Beauty*. Rose hips are useful for making soothing teas.

Cookbooks and interior decoration books, ancient and contemporary, illustrate how important herbs are in French living.

Animals, birds, reptiles, and amphibians are admired all over France, and the French are famous for making all animals delicious to eat. Little creatures of the woods are cherished. *Herisson* (hedgehog), *lapins* (rabbits), *grenouilles* (frogs), and *escargots* (snails) are admired in sauces, as well as in stories. Turtle soup is a delicacy. Many kinds of birds live in France, too. The seacoasts and rich countryside provide good food and nesting places for the birds. The *merles* (blackbirds) sing sweetly as do nightingales and doves. Pheasants, geese, duck, chicken, and now, turkey are main agricultural products for the French market. Animals living all over France have found their way to the French dinner plate.

Additionally, as in all countries, animals are kept in the home as pets. In France, dogs outnumber cats as favorites. *Liberté, égalité, et fraternité* (Liberty, equality, and fraternity) is truly a revolutionary slogan—it seems to apply even to dogs! Dogs peek out of shopping baskets; dogs walk into stores; dogs sit patiently at sidewalk cafés. They follow their humans everywhere and are a part of the community. The French poodle comes in all sizes from miniature to giant. In France, animals are everywhere—in meals, in art, with families, in small apartments, at parks, in puppet shows, on sidewalks, and in the wild.

In Your Classroom

Make a sachet. Simple sachets can be made using paper washing cloths, a stapler, and a variety of dried herbs and flowers. Have each student fold one paper washing cloth in half. The student should then fold the sides in and staple them closed to make a pocket. Students can select dried rose petals, rosemary leaves, mint leaves, or lavender flowers to put inside the pocket. (You may want to purchase these fresh and dry them in the classroom.) Then they can staple the top of the bag closed. Sachets can be placed in a clothes drawer or under a pillow. *Bonne nuit!* Good night! Sleep sweetly!

Plant a mint garden. Bring in mint cuttings and allow students to place them in water until roots grow. They can then plant the cuttings in pots or in a garden. They will love to watch the mint thrive! Pick leaves to steep for tea, to rub on a table for a fresh smell, or to dip in sugar syrup for elegant cake decorations.

A French garden

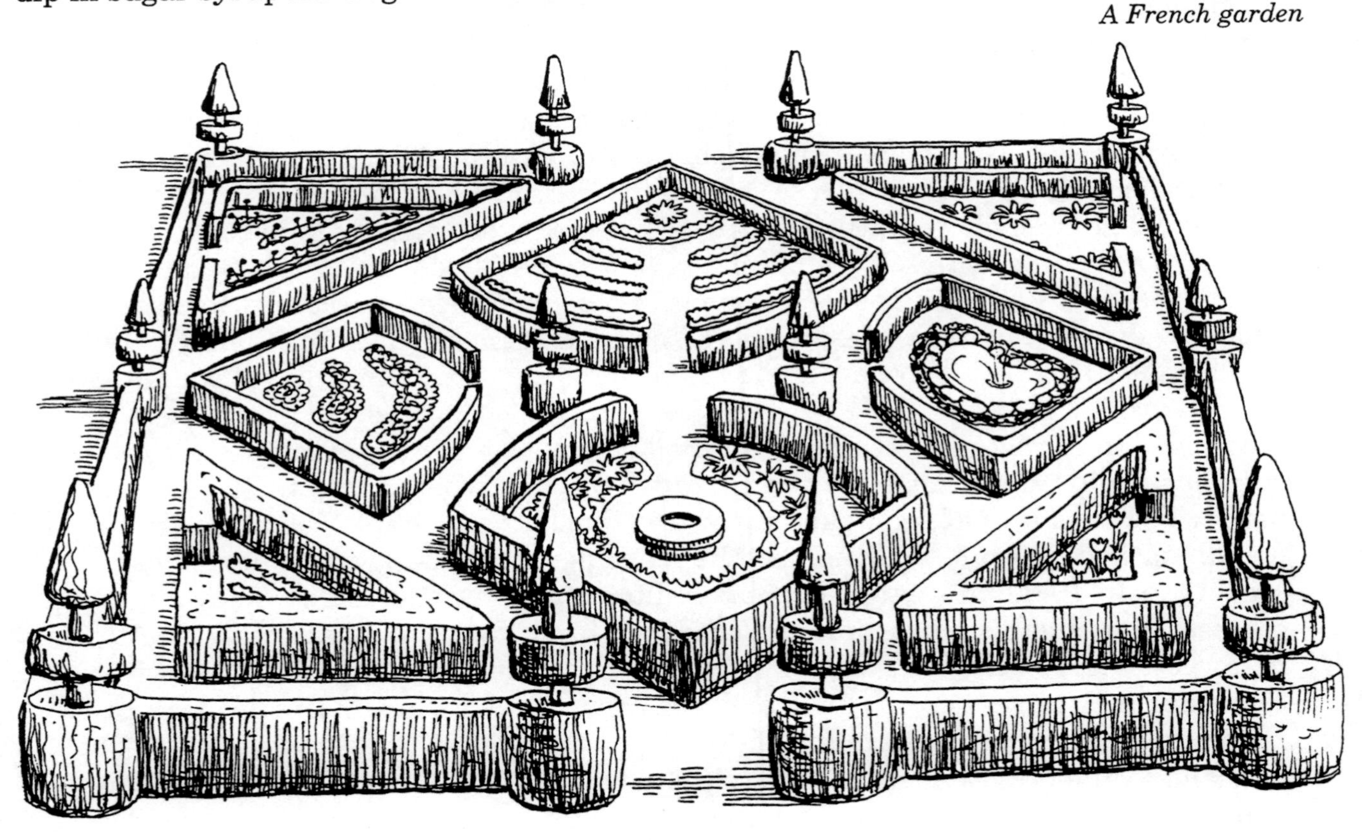

Read French animal stories. Many delightful animal stories have been translated from the French. Ludwig Bemelman's *Madeline* and Laurent de Brunhoff's *Babar the Elephant* series are loved around the world. Madeline's adventures have delighted children for over 50 years. *Madeline's Rescue* involves a cherished dog. Read the series and enjoy rhyme, pictures, and the adventures of Madeline and "the old house in Paris, all covered with vines." In the Babar books, one glimpses a gentle society ruled by benevolent elephants. The detailed illustrations and moralistic stories make them engaging tales.

Have students write and illustrate a story about a pet, real or imagined. They can include the French words for dog (*le chien*), cat (*le chat*), bird (*l'oiseau*), or fish (*le poisson*).

Fabulous Foods

Food in France is *magnifique* (magnificent). The taste and appearance of food and the act of eating are both very important to the French. Purchasing food can be as elaborate a process as the preparation of the meal itself. In big cities and in small villages, outdoor markets are held weekly. Local farmers bring cheese, pâté, fresh meat, sausages, fruits, vegetables, shell fish, and fresh breads from their farms in the countryside. At these *marché,* one can wander the town square munching on fresh bread and cheese. Throughout the week, the French shop daily at local specialty shops for the freshest produce: *le boucherie* (butcher shop), *la boulangerie* (bakery), *le marchand de légumes* (green grocer) *le poissonnerie* (fishmonger), *le charcuterie* (delicatessan) and *la pâtisserie* (pastry shop). Shopping is also a social activity during which patrons and merchants can share local news. Only recently have large supermarkets, like those in the U.S., opened in France. These *supermarchés* are not likely to become as popular as the traditional specialty shops. A market basket or string bag is an attractive necessity for regular shopping duties. Children bring home the bread for lunch or pick up a fancy cake for the Sunday meal. Meals involve everyone in the shopping, preparing, and of course, eating.

Mealtimes in France are not taken lightly. The day begins with breakfast—*le petit déjeuner.* Children usually have a large cup of cocoa in which to dip their morning baguette. They may eat cereal and toast, and drink orange juice. The bread for the meal is usually picked up from the bakery in the morning. After breakfast, children leave for school. About 10:00, they stop for a *goûter,* literally a "taste" or snack. They might eat cookies, fruit, small sandwiches, or a chocolate bar before going back to work. At noon, many children go home for lunch. *Le déjeuner* is a family meal which begins with soup, continues with a meat or fish dish, and finishes with a dessert. After the meal, children return to school. Along with many adults across the nation, they stop their work between 3:30 and 4:30 for another snack. Chocolate–filled pastries (*pain au chocolat*), a piece of fruit, or a big chunk of baguette satisfies until dinner. On their way home, children may purchase the evening's bread. Later in the evening, the family gathers for *dîner,* often a light meal in three courses. Before going to bed, children enjoy one more snack of bread, fruit, or chocolate.

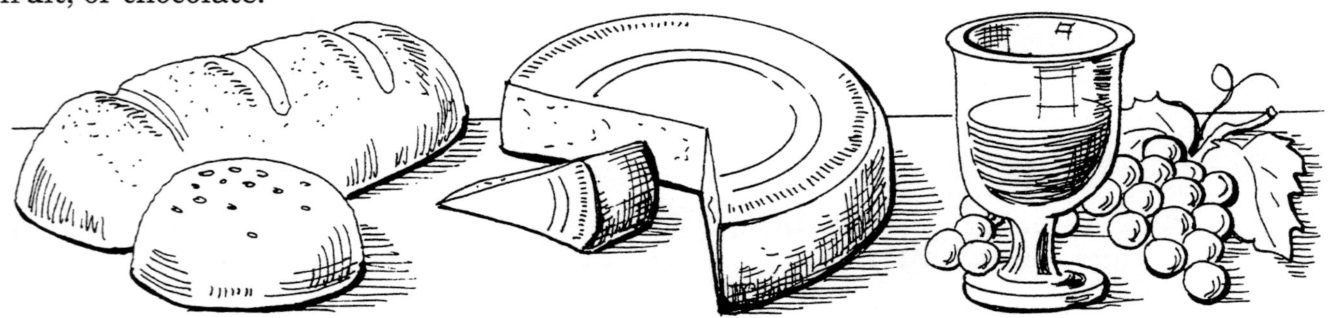

In Your Classroom

Set up a market. Make signs for French specialty stores: *boucherie, pâtisserie, boulangerie, charcuterie, poissionaire,* and *marchand de légumes.* Give students time to prepare foods from play dough. They can then go shopping and practice math using some simple French sentences.

Combien de francs pour_____?	How much money for_____?
Merci, madame / monsieur.	Thank you, madame/sir.
Au revoir, madame / monsieur.	Good–bye, madame/sir.

Sample French food. Simple French recipes will extend students' taste of France! You may want to research some of the many excellent French cookbooks available for popular ragouts, quiches, and potages. Bring in a collection of cookbooks for your Explore France! area. Students will notice how decorative the dishes are. Note the metric units used in the recipes and assist students in converting recipes to the English system. Plan an outdoor picnic or formal dinner, complete with hand–lettered menus, to celebrate your flair for fabulous French foods. *Bon appétit!* Eat well!

Baguettes
Purchase long sourdough loaves or make your own from frozen breads. Serve hot. You may want to include toppings such as cheese, butter, or jam.

***Les Fromages* (Cheeses)**
France is famous for its cheeses. Some say there is a different cheese for each day of the year, but there are probably more than 365 kinds of cheese available in France. Purchase a variety of cheeses to sample in the classroom. You may want to look for *chèvre* (goat's cheese), *Camenbert* and *Brie* (round creamy cheeses), and blue cheeses (in varying degrees of pungency). Hard cheeses, soft cheeses, sweet cheeses, and salty cheeses are all part of daily life in France. All these cheeses go very well with the national treasure of French bread.

Crêpes
Prepare a thin pancake batter. Cook in a crêpe pan. Flip and roll with jelly, butter, or powdered sugar. An easy favorite!

***Langue Du Chat* (Cat's Tongues)**
Cream together 1/2 cup butter with 1/2 cup white sugar. Add 1 egg, 1/2 teaspoon vanilla or almond extract, or lemon rind. Beat in 3/4 cup flour into mixture. Drop cookies onto a greased cookie sheet and bake at 375°F for about 6 minutes. These delicate buttery cookies will have slightly browned edges.

Meringues
Separate 5 egg whites and beat until frothy. Add a pinch of cream of tartar (optional) and 1/2 teaspoon almond or vanilla extract. Slowly add about 1 cup sugar until the batter is stiff and shiny. (Depending on the humidity, more or less sugar is required to make the egg whites stiff. Use less rather than more.) Add food coloring or sugar sprinkles. Drop into little mounds on an ungreased cookie sheet. Bake at 250°F for about an hour. Serve *á la mode* (with ice cream or fruit) or eat plain. Enjoy these elegant, inexpensive, and fun French treats!

***Les Pommes des Tartes* (Apple Tarts)**
Prepare a crust by creaming 3/4 cup butter with 1/3 cup sugar. Add 1 egg, 2 cups flour, and 1/2 teaspoon salt. Press dough into a pie pan. Chill for several hours. Peel and slice 10 apples. Sprinkle with sugar and lemon juice. Arrange apple slices in circles in the crust. Bake at 350°F until apples are slightly soft and crust is golden brown.

***Galette des Rois* (Cake of Kings)**
Double the recipe for Cat's Tongues and bake 2 large pie–shaped cookies. Cool. Spread one cookie with sweetened almond paste. Tuck a *fève* (tiny porcelain figure, raisin, or bean) somewhere in the paste. Then place the second cookie on top of the first. Cut and serve. Whoever gets the *fève* should be crowned king or queen of the party.

***Pain au Chocolat* (Bread with Chocolate)**
Buy croissants, fresh or frozen. Insert chocolate chips, and heat until chocolate is melted. Or take a baguette, and spread melted chocolate on it. Enjoy as a snack!

Language and Expressions

French is spoken worldwide by more than 90 million people. It has been an international language of diplomacy for centuries. Former French colonies in Africa and Asia continue to speak French, as do French Canadians and some Swiss. In Europe and the Americas, many people speak French as a second language. In France, citizens are dedicated to their own language. The French Academy is an organization of intellectuals that exists to keep the language pure and correct. Although they discourage people from using English words, several favorites such as *le week end, le pique–nique,* and *le homework* are used. French language study is the core of the school's curriculum. Throughout France, it is considered very important to speak, write, and read French properly, elegantly, and articulately. Politeness is important in language, as well as in manners. Using *"madame"* or *"monsieur"* in saying hello, answering a question, or making a request is considered proper. Foreigners are often chagrined when their French is corrected by bus conductors, bread sellers, and friends. Speaking well is considered the mark of a French person.

French is a phonetic language structured much like English. The alphabet is the same although pronounced differently. Nouns have gender, indicated by the masculine "le" and the feminine "la," and adjectives and possessives reflect the gender. Most verbs follow regular conjugations. French is based on Latin. Some say it is only Latin spoken with the prevalent French cold stopping up the nose and resulting in a twang!

French pronunciation is fun and easy!

a is like fAther
o is like mOth
au or **eaux** is like O in Open
ç is soft as in Cider
è or **ê** is like sEt
i is like E in Eat
r should be rolled
ch is like sh
é is like the A in cAke
oi is pronounced WA
qu sounds like a K

A final **e** is silent. Final consonants are also silent, except for a final **C, R, F,** or **L.** (Remember the consonants of CaReFuL!)

In Your Classroom

Get a tape of the French alphabet and enjoy singing the ABC song in French. Encourage students to use French dictionaries and books in the Explore France! area. Ask them to look up the French words for common items, and then to label the items. Help them practice saying the French words and phrases.

French Vocabulary

Common Words

les enfants	children
le garçon	boy
la fille	girl
l'ami	friend who is a boy
l'amie	friend who is a girl
le père	father
la mère	mother
la soeur	sister
le frère	brother
le bébé	baby
le chien	dog
le chat	cat
la table	table
la chaise	chair
le crayon	pencil
la canteen	cafeteria
la salle de classe	classroom
l'ordinateur	computer
la maitresse	teacher
le professeur	teacher
l'école	school
la toilette or *W.C.*	bathroom

Numbers

un	1
deux	2
trois	3
quatre	4
cinq	5
six	6
sept	7
huit	8
neuf	9
dix	10

Colors

rouge	red
bleu or *bleue*	blue
vert or *verte*	green
jaune	yellow
noir or *noire*	black
blanc or *blanche*	white

Expressions

Bonjour, Madame / Monsieur	Hello
Au revoir, Madame / Monsieur	Good–bye
Merci	Thank you
S'il vous plait	Please
Comment vous appellez–vous?	What is your name?
Je m'appelle ____.	My name is ____.
Quel age avez–vous?	How old are you?
J'ai _____ans.	I am____ years old.
C'est magnifique!	It's magnificent!
C'est dommage	Too bad

Sports and Games

French children spend a lot of time playing in parks. Even in the cities, there are many green areas with trees, carousels, sand pits for games, slides, and fountains. For example, Luxembourg Gardens in Paris has splendid statues, wide ponds for sailing boats, sandy paths for people, dogs, and ponies to walk on, and spaces for picnics, reading, intense discussions, and impromptu concerts. Parks surround castles, office buildings, and churches. They are in the midst of industrial areas and block housing. Every weekend after dinner, families take walks to digest and to be together.

Bicycling is a way of transportation for many people. A light two–wheel bicycle is easier to park than a big four–wheel car. Bike racing is a serious sport. People in bicycle clubs practice all year long for *Le Tour de France,* an international bike race which takes place in July. Children collect souvenirs of their favorite riders and teams, and winners are instant heroes.

Soccer, known in France as *footbal,* is the favorite national sport. It is played year round, at school, in parks, and on formal teams. Swimming, tennis, basketball, and other team programs are popular, too. *Boules,* a game of lawn bowling played in the park, and *pelota,* a game similar to handball, are common in some areas. Fitness is now considered to be an important health goal for adults and children alike.

Children's games seem the same the world over. Children fill recess and free time with jump rope (*sauter à la corde*), jacks (*osselet*), hopscotch (*la marelle*), and hide–and–seek (*cache–cache*), as well as with tag and many witty word games.

In Your Classroom

Play two simple games with young children: *Pouce–Pouce* (Thumb–Thumb) and *Chemin de Fer* (Train).

***Pouce–Pouce* (Thumb–Thumb)**

Make a fist and say:
Pouce, pouce, petit pouce, es–tu là?

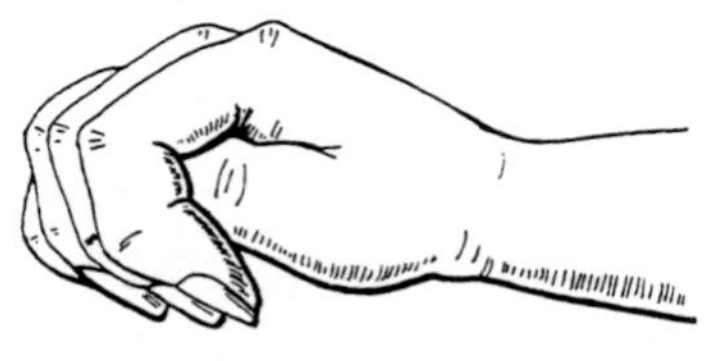

Thumb, thumb, little thumb, are you there?

Bring thumb out and say:
Voila, voila, je suis là.

Here, here, I am here.

Then say:
Petit doigt, petit doigt, es–tu là?

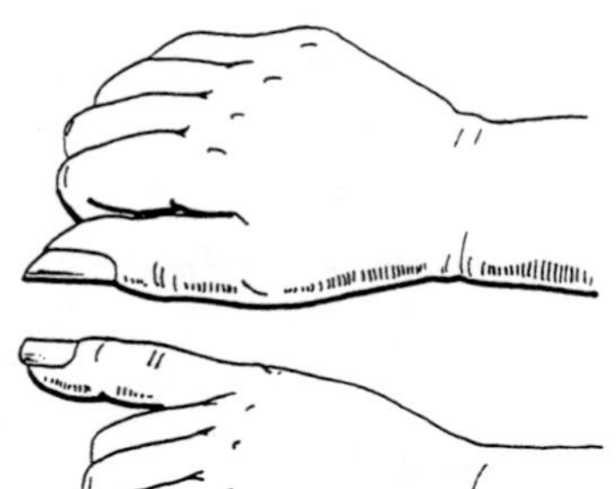

Little finger, little finger, are you there?

Bring little finger out and say:
Voilà, voilà, je suis là.

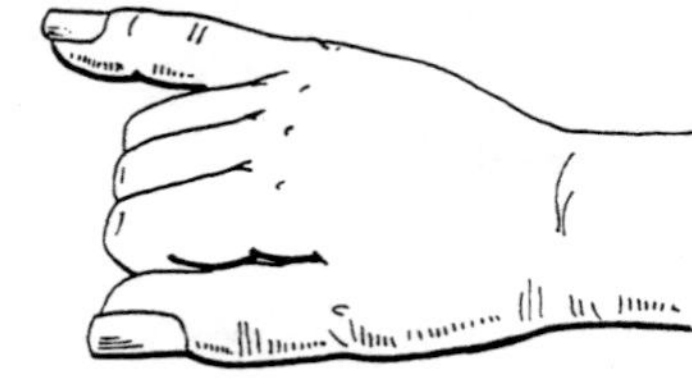

Here, here, I am here.

***Chemins de Fer* (Trains)**

Have children form a single–file line and then walk in one big circle to act out a train wheel turning. Chant the words below. Select one child to walk on the outside of the circle as the conductor, touching each child gently as he or she passes. On *"RÉGARDEZ"* or "LOOK," everyone should stop and the last child to be tapped becomes the conductor.

Roulez, roulez, chemins de fer,	Roll, roll, trains.
Roulez comme ça marche,	Roll as we walk,
comme ça marche.	as we walk.
Roulez roulez chemins de fer,	Roll, roll, trains.
Roulez comme ça marche.	Roll as we walk.
RÉGARDEZ!	LOOK!

On the globe, find all the countries which participate in World Cup soccer. Where will the World Cup be held this year?

Find out who is in the Tour de France and trace the route of the race on a map. Imagine what it would be like to ride day after day with crowds waiting for you along the road. Illustrate some aspect of the race.

Creative Arts

Art is part of daily life in France. Knowing how to appreciate many different forms of art is important. Children are taught at school and by example. Art fills the culture from cooking to home decorating, from fine arts to gardening. School field trips, as well as Sunday afternoon family walks, are directed toward knowing about and appreciating different aspects of French creative arts.

Early Art

The earliest known art created in France is seen in prehistoric cave paintings. The first paintings were discovered in Lascaux, when a boy and his dog fell into a cave. Careful archaeological research revealed delicate scenes painted on cave walls more than thirty thousand years ago. Paintings and drawings of hundreds of horses, as well as reindeer, bison, and other wild animals were found in the Lascaux cave and later in other caves in France. Many archaeologists think they were drawn for magic or religious ceremonies, or to symbolize the animals early people hunted.

Thousands of years later, the Romans inhabited France (58 B.C.–400 A.D.). They built temples, amphitheaters, civic buildings, and roads in France. Their style, now known as the classical style, can still be seen in many places in France. The style is characterized by tall, heavy columns and rounded stone arches.

Art of the Medieval Period

After the collapse of the Roman Empire, there was a period of several hundred years (early Medieval Period) when little art was created. Then Charles the Great built his empire and attempted to revive Roman civilization. He encouraged architects, painters, writers, and other artists. Catholicism was spreading across France, and many new cathedrals and castles were built. At first they were built of thick and heavy stone, and as a result, these buildings were very dark inside. Eventually, technology advanced and a Gothic style developed. Buttresses and pointed arches allowed architects to design thinner walls. They built taller and taller buildings, and included more windows to bring lots of light into their cathedrals. Splendid stained glass windows, often showing religious images, were created for these cathedrals.

During the Medieval Period, many manuscripts, namely the Bible and other prayer books, were copied in beautiful handwriting and were illustrated with beautifully colored pictures. Literature of this time consisted mostly of romantic poetry set to music. Nobles would often hire troubadours to sing and entertain the people living in the castle. Some troubadours wandered from place to place entertaining anyone who would listen. Epic poems about lovers and knights were also common.

Tapestries, or woven pictures, also developed as an art form during this time. They were needed to cover cold, drafty castle walls. The Normandy Bayeux tapestry depicting the 1066 invasion of England by the Norman Duke, William the Conqueror, and the splendid Apocalypse tapestry of Angers demonstrate how tapestries became functional works of art that recorded history. Today, tapestries are still made in France, but usually to cover less grandiose objects, such as purses, belts, and small walls.

From Medieval times to the present, French handiwork has been admired. Kings and queens, nobles and common people all dressed to fit their occupations and to decorate their rooms. Elegant designs and intricate stitches continue to make French clothing, furniture, and accessories famous and desirable. Paris is one of the world's centers for high fashion.

Marie Antoinette

Revolutionary Art

France has been a cradle for the fine arts, too. Art movements and artists found inspiration and support in France. People came from around the world to paint, sculpt, design, study, and admire art in all forms. During the Renaissance in the 16th and 17th centuries, artists, musicians, dramatists, writers, and scholars were drawn to the royal court. Under royal and aristocratic patronage, the arts flourished. Music of Lully and Rameau and their followers were encouraged. Writers and philosophers such as Voltaire, Rousseau, and Diderot inspired readers and incited discussion. Racine, Corneille, and Molière, three famous dramatists, broadened the French language with their stories, and mirrored an increasingly stressed society.

Many genres of art originated in France. Art of the Renaissance, highly influenced by the Italians, depicted mostly religious scenes and portraits of aristocrats and royalty. However, with the French Revolution came new thinking and new styles. As the clergy and royalty and aristocracy lost power, they no longer sponsored artists. As a result, artists began to experiment more, choosing new subjects—often common people in scenes of everyday life—new techniques, and new ways of representation.

Art became studies in color, shadow, light, line, and pattern, rather than the beautified, idealized portraits and religious scenes of earlier art. Realism, surrealism, cubism, and impressionism are words we have come to associate with 19th and 20th century art.

The late 19th century and early 20th century saw a flowering of art. Artists flocked to France to participate in what is now called the Impressionist period. Artists such as Degas, Toulouse Lautrec, Monet, Van Gogh, Renoir, Picasso, and Matisse continued to experiment and stretch imagination and technique through the 20th century: Van Gogh's strong lines and bright oil colors created a powerful impression of the south of France. Monet's garden provided a whole career for him. Although Monet was a prolific painter, the works he is most famous for are the huge canvases depicting his garden at Giverny. He chose to paint the same scenes over and over, each time at a different time of day, thus illustrating the essential ingredient of light, as well as form. Matisse was involved in many of the 20th century art movements. His cutouts came toward the end of his life and make a strong contrast to the impressionist philosophy. Picasso created in a variety of media. His paintings, drawings, sculptures, costumes, and collages contribute to the richness of 20th century art. One of the more intriguing styles he experimented with was cubism. Picasso took figures and broke them at different angles to create non–traditional forms of representation.

In the 20th century, France has continued to lead the world in the arts. French culture teaches, practices, and highly values the artistic view of life. From castles to cakes, much of French art is "frou frou." Castles are decorated elaborately and cakes glory in swirls and arcs of candied fruit or wisps of chocolate curls. Contemporary movements have produced utilitarian buildings, like the *Gare Montparnasse* (train station) and *Centre Pompidou* (museum), which glory in their structural points. The *Louvre,* a world famous art museum in Paris, pairs a Renaissance palace with a late 20th century glass pyramid. In the Paris subway, people ride the swift, sleek, metallic Metro trains and use the Metro's 19th century art–nouveau decorative gates. Maintaining and preserving the old, while constantly reinventing how people use and decorate space is a way of life in France. Creative art movements from ancient days to the present have shaped France's history and still impact the whole world.

In Your Classroom

Have students use sidewalk chalk to draw scenes from their everyday life. Compare the drawings with cave paintings.

Have students research and illustrate fashions from various time periods. Create a "History of French Fashions" book.

In the fashion industry, dolls have been fitted with tiny versions of the latest fashions. Use Barbie dolls and create your own miniature fashion show.

Display works by various French artists. Let students copy the styles. They could use markers to imitate Van Gogh, watercolors for Monet, and objects made of construction paper that are cut and scrambled to resemble Picasso.

Listen to recordings of medieval church music and Renaissance court music, as well as to the music of Lully, Rameau, and Debussy.

Additional Resources

There is a plethora of books about France available. The public library or any bookstore offers dictionaries, story books, and reference books for children as well as adults. Canadian teacher resources and publishing houses are good resources for books in French. Many favorite authors are translated into French. Children's illustrated dictionaries are excellent tools for research. Enjoy your exploring!

Aliki. *The King's Day: Louis XIV of France.* Thomas Y. Crowell, 1989. (ISBN 0–690–04588–3) An illustrated rhymed history of the Sun King.

Axworthy, Anni. *Anni's Diary of France.* Whispering Coyote Press, Inc., 1994. (ISBN 1–879085–58–5) A journal with drawings and children–referenced activities.

Bemelmans, Ludwig. *Madeline* books. Viking Press. (ISBN 0590–75942–6)

Bjork, Christina. *Linnea in Monet's Garden.* R & S Books. (ISBN 91–29–58314–4) A delightful story with drawings and photos of Monet, his garden, and a French trip.

Blackwoood, Alan and Brigitte Chosey. *Countries of the World: France.* Bookwright Press, 1988. (ISBN 0–531–18186–3) A reference book with photographs.

Brunhoff, Jean de. *Babar* books. Random House. (ISBN 0–394–80576–3)

Cole, Ann et al. *Children Are Children Are Children.* Little, Brown & Co. (ISBN 0–316–15114–9) An activity approach to exploring, Brazil, France, Iran, Japan, Nigeria and the former USSR, and still the best activity and short reference resource for teachers.

Kowalchik and Hylton, eds. *Rodale's Illustrated Encyclopedia of Herbs.* Rodale Press, 1987.

Macaulay, David. *Cathedral.* Houghton–Mifflin. (ISBN 0–395–17513–5)

———. *Castle.* Houghton–Mifflin. (ISBN 0–395–25784–0) Macaulay's books are super for children to explore as they are full of diagrams and fascinating facts.

McCully, Emily Arnold. *Mirette of the High Wire.* Scholastic. (ISBN 0–590–47693–9) A charming story of Paris, high wires, and a special friendship.

Montaufier, Poupa. *The Summer at Grandmother's House.* Carolrhoda Books, 1985. (ISBN 0–87614–238–2) A book of drawings and text about French families and the French countryside.

Munro, Dixie. *Inside / Outside Book of Paris.* Dutton's Children's Books, 1992. (ISBN 0–525–44863–2) A book with drawings and text about the French capital.

Saint–Exupery, Antoine. *The Little Prince.* Harcourt Brace and World, Inc., 1943. (ISBN 0–15–246503–0) A classic French fantasy.

NOTE: *Cinderella, Sleeping Beauty, Little Red Riding Hood, Princess Furball,* and *Beauty and the Beast* are fairy tales of French origin. Search for different versions of the same tale, in English or from different cultures.

Day and Night

Written by Celia Erwin

Harcourt
Supplemental Publishers
Rigby • Steck-Vaughn

www.steck-vaughn.com

In the day, the sun shines.
It is light outside.

At night, the moon shines.
It is dark outside.

Sky

On most days, the sky is blue.
We can see clouds in the sky.

At night, the sky is black.
We can see stars in the sky.

Flowers

In the day, flowers get light from the sun.
Some flowers open in the light.

At night, some flowers close up.
They stay closed in the dark.

Birds

In the day, most birds are awake.
They open their wings in the sun.

At night, most birds go to sleep.
They close their eyes in the dark.

Dogs

In the day, most dogs are awake.
They run and play in the sun.

At night, most dogs go to sleep.
They close their eyes in the dark.

Towns

In the day, most towns are busy.
The stores are full of people.

At night, most towns are quiet.
The stores close, and people go home.

You

What do you do in the day?
Do you run and play in the sun?

What do you do at night?
Do you close your eyes and go to sleep?

Index